AF480793

Ribs
&
Wonder

YOU PUBLISHING

Published by You Publishing, LLC

All Rights reserved.

Library of Congress Cataloging-in-Publication Data

Name: Locke, Kyra, author.

Title: Ribs & Wonder, A poetry collection / Kyra Locke

Description: First edition. | San Pedro, California: You Publishing, LLC, 2022

Identifiers: LCCN 2022903748 (print) ISBN 9798985491579 (hardback) |

ISBN 9798985491593 (ebook) |

Published in the United States of America

10 9 8 7 6 5 4 3 2 1

www.youpublishing.shop

IG: @KyratheWriter

Editors: Suzanne Ondrus, Kyra Locke

Book Design:
Cover: Michael Corvin, Touqeer Shahid
Interior: Kyra Locke, Asha M.

Photo Credits:
Cover: Sarder Kamangar
Center: Steve Ragland
Author: Jonathan Marlow

* The cover photo of Kyra was taken on a train platform in Hikone, Japan - January, 1998. The center proof sheet reflects examples of photos Kyra submitted to Johnson Publishing Company to be considered for the 2001-2002 Ebony Fashion Fair Tour. Kyra was one of 12 models chosen.

CONTENTS

Ribs & Wonder

Lasso

lasso light where the body bends
relax into the glow it lends
watch peace pearl on waters skin
it is the balm that longs to mend

lasso moon where her light extends
faith begins where worry ends
sip fullness from the silver wind
she is the light that shines to mend

lasso peace where branches bend
climb the beams that know no end
green and lush the joy within
it is the balm that longs to mend

Backrush

she holds a million midnights in her belly
and a field of stars on her skin
the life that wallows in her womb
is the same they hold within

he is the man here
she is the woman there

they come to Pacific shores bare and burdened
believing in her vastness
the fetch of her waves allows their hopes to meet at the center

pause surrounds their shoulders
dreaming away agenda and posture

they ponder her abundance
wanting purpose to emerge from her bars
appearing unto her whole
only to feel like specks in her dunes

her offering   as consistent as her waves
seashells belched in the tides
she awaits the patter of feet to collect them

on both shores they find similar ones
for there are no roads or dams to
dictate life beneath the ebbing

his   decorations for his desk
hers   an offering for her altar

they send their prayers out
with the backrush

hers   to the kami of heaven and Earth
his   to the God that created them

Poem Om

Colliding creations of imagination
and thought
inspired by opportunities
within suffering

Examining the gravity
of culture and righteousness
the grin of grinding
the ache of dying

Melodic texture
belting conjecture
a lecture in elegant bias

Confessions
and
dreaming
of all that is seeming to
be visceral and true

A well of hope within all of us
what shall it render
what shall it rust

Apexes of the mundane
inspiration that sustains beyond
bonds that wane

Every poem is meant to be
just like the beautiful twisted lives
behind them

Energy and impulse
ink and thought
binding pages
across the ages

What is written is
what wanted to be
and what wants to be is
written

So that in years to come
either love will be its lyric or
bitterness its mirror

Javelin

with all my might
I throw you

right out of my hand
doesn't matter if I'm torn within

doesn't matter if it's
against the wind

away from me
diseased integrity

pierce every dishonorable word
on your way to stabbing the Earth

with all my might
I watch you fade

a beam of light in
an abandoned cave

to a life we could have made
to a love that could have aged

I wave

She

she
captured
love
on
a
wing
of
a
humming bird
alighted
on
the
lines
of
history

she
was
a
revolutionary
well
before
clay
claimed
its
color

Deception

deep in the middle of square shoulders
a whisper crawled within itself and died
doubled over
clinching her naps
she strangled the kinks that composed her crown
and sent her voice walking in the distance

infected honor dripped from her pores
bleeding into the tongues of her children
Eden is no longer my home
no longer my home
is no longer my home

weeping and groaning   she summoned the
hand of justice and balanced her scales
for she could squint
and way over yonder see
her children shackled to the certainty of sin

feeling out the yield of a newborn Earth
one foot in front of the other
carrying perfection to an unhappy place
her toes clutched the substance of their birth

teardrops were the Earth's first rain
deception her first pain
her burdens challenged the banks of God's pardon

her ribbed body made wonderment out of
the utterance of creation
freshly kneaded hands and feet
elbows and her torso mimicked the
limbs of trees

teetering to the rhythms of mist
and to the song of the newly formed seas

beauty opened its eyes to her
when she awakened against
the simmering Earth
but as her clay hands
clutched the clay beneath her
she sent a whisper up to God

forgive me Nyame   Nyame forgive me
forgive me Nyame   Nyame receive me

it's that I'm understanding Eve

Before I Was

wondering if this world spinning 'round
seen another like me
not perpetuating the notion of reincarnation but
when I dream of faces and places of old
I believe somewhere in there lay
souls that saw like I see
directing feet to venture where I went
retracing the same patterns of dream-making
and soul searching
whose thoughts traveled the heights of depression
whose misery visited the depths of joy and cried

These Are the Dead Who Know

urns and graves
house their remains
while oceans and rivers
hold the whispers of
exhaled completion
the ageless memory of humanity

our sacred dead

who walked the miles and fields
who breathed the air of the Serengeti
and savored the city of Jasmine
those who stood in storefronts and schoolrooms
brides and grooms bastards and priests
princes and thieves

they are aware
of any validity in any religion
those institutions of absolutes that intersect
and parallel and circle around truth

yes   these are the dead who know

standing in every direction
exhaling longitude into vacuums
wormholes and rituals   weaving nets to capture story
they are the mosaics the Earth cradled and nurtured

eons of lovely conversation and song
tapestries hanging from neolithic bones
let oceans and rivers hold their whispers
while land articulates their gait
let oceans and rivers hold their whispers
while Earth immortalizes their fate

Acquire

we did not come to Earth to acquire
control however difficult it seems
the gnawing of human desire

websites and aisles allure to explore
the unrelenting screeching of greed
it fights to never expire

whether self-serve or work-for-hire
both attempt to appease the need
the gnawing of human desire

closets and drawers are added for more
with racks and stacks swinging from beams
if only the ceilings were higher

trinkets and balms and trendy attire
thrill and dazzle and glow they gleam
and fight to never expire

the tugs the pulls the internal wars
checked out and ever so tone-deaf we seem
we did not come to Earth to acquire
or drown in human desire

The Dance

we choose to dance when the rain comes to visit
a window of pleasure we measure its worth
its shine on shoulders is something exquisite

strati straddle the hurdle of lightning
scratching and thrashing the skies cry for Earth
we choose to dance when rain comes to visit

dangerous   luxurious   hmm   which is it
we mull it over as we sip tea in Perth
the air is crisp there   just something exquisite

an umbrella   how counter-enlightening
expected   a usual refusal to purge
we choose to dance when rain comes to visit

even if it falls for days or just snippets
how long will we waltz with this floundering urge
until the mundane morphs into exquisite

drenching just kneads and releases the tightening
we know just what water will cause to emerge
we choose to dance when the rain comes to visit
its shine on shoulders is something exquisite

The Itting of It

couches and candlelight
a night of Shiraz and
William Grant Still

it is the feel and hope and dream of it
how it dances and eludes penetrates and
opens

evading and fading while decades
play in the film of memory

simmering coloring morning
one chance to get it right and feeling solid in
the getting

hold on to it

let it sweat and cry and drip and dry and
hang and swing and get lost in everything

it's the *itting* of it or
whatever you call it

wallow in the mood and tone of it

make it a night of Cabernet
couches and candlelight
William composing a moment a
hundred years in the making

Still... is still...

my melodic representation
of
him

Compatibility Some Say

neon lights blink

Bahamadia rhymes through tenor
I am collapsed in a wingback   my limbs its fringe spilling over
and sprawled
the Neo-soul of it all

a rock-a-bye presence
of fake velvet and crocheted warmth
my hands brush the table just beyond my head and
wouldn't you know it   a book of matches from 736 Java

an immediate flashback
a table for two   me and you   two mirages
reflecting fake naturalness
fidgeting with feigned cool

to my chagrin my creased concealer and smudged mascara
flirted with you through black lights
while you tapped your feet to the beat of *The Sweetest Thing*

two weeks ago would return you to me and leave me swinging
from your charm
'cause see
you have me going like gotcha jokes
like travel   and I'm willing   to go   the distance

Bahamadia   *does everything men do revolve around women*
'cause he doesn't even see me
everything about me says see me   behold me
be like this chair and take the heaviness out of my weight
get your walking stick and join in this here journey

as we orbit   I wonder   where are you
you're definitely not on my corner or climbing my steps or
exiting the Lodge freeway at my exit
you seem emotionless   out of touch   not picking up what I'm
putting down
all day long I gaze   chin up   eyes straining for clues
there's the moon in the daylight
and   oh look   it's raining

Compatibility Some Say (remix)

you

are

old letters and poems

you

a

breeze of lilac

in a wave of burning sage

so pleasant to think of as we age

our places our moments

painted in laughter

we leaned into being free

and bonded over creativity

we were a vibe and

so was our sanctuary

Cafe Mahogany

somewhat of a reliquary

where neon lights blinked

a wellspring of offerings

Thursday night poetry

music and cuddling

sipping and flirting

an energy that was everything

hand claps and toe taps

a vibe that was right on time

we sat closely hip-to-hip

being elevated by beats and rhymes

everything flowed

our personal dream-world where

we felt free to express

emote and suggest

embracing what the world

called us to digest

togetherness

yes

look at us

we old

and life

has been

real

and

real

real good

yes us

we are

a light drizzle on a hot day

the moonlight on an ocean wave

where memories and longevity

cascade we are

old letters and poems

we are timeless

and time all wrapped into

one

Voodoo

yonder sits a gypsy stationed at a blinking light a   jinx
in motion   she keeps tabs on the pressures of the Earth
Bertha knows it's not necessary to name her head crazy so she
continues to watch you   so do I   I know that particular
loudness when thoughts discombobulate   bruising
themselves in efforts to locate exits in a mazed mind   I saw
you   sauntering down   you side-walked through a crowd
while Bertha was perched atop an old trunk imported from the
blue side of Guinea   she bedazzles Wolfgang   a native of the
streets   he returns to his cardboard abode   lays his head
flat in a rainbow of oil and yesterday's piss and attempts to
settle the war   the pool wasn't *too* big   didn't smell too
badly   if you press pause then silence your feet   turn your
head to see what's behind your body   you will find her eyes
fixed on your silhouette   your pendulous thoughts oscillate
I sit at the base of a blinking crosswalk light   programming
myself   *and to the republic for which it stands one nation
under God*   observing the hex you've succumb to   all this
time I thought I was your obsession

Boomerang

I'm a reminder of what he had.

She's a reminder of what he didn't want.

How you gon' be married for 20 years & he ain't
never rubbed your feet?

her feet

be like

Injera Tapalapa Sugar Bread dough in his hands

needing the knead of his hands

the type of telepathy that calms her chi

he knows her feet intimately

a squeeze a kiss a taste

nothing like

her feet in his hands

have you ever had that—

monogamy and the rubbing of feet   regularly

tender   pure   dependable love

I do *ain't got nothing on a foot rub*

Eye Haiku

beauty named her soul

leaped underneath oppression

smiled and slit its throat

she called me nigger

white Range Rover changing lanes

white silicone lips

29
29A
30
30A
0
35
608 21
36
AGFA APX 100
35
35A
36
36A

For John and Eunice Johnson: Thank You

first woman to rock locks
on an Ebony Fashion Fair runway

walk
twirl
pose
sway

skincare for me
make up for me
everywhere I look
faces look just like me

MCs
stylists
models
drivers

a legacy built around
black beauty

how we look
how we love
how we flow
how we speak
how we vibe
how we glide
how we glow
how we think

innovators
motivators
shining
in whatever we decide to be

and ooh
can we strut

Right Now

racism
the gangrene
of society right now

protest
the language
of the world right now

peace
is the dream
of humanity right now

breath
is the plea
of the dying right now

They See

in the midst of life threatening conditions
the mission of human decency was not lost

every protestor had an elder praying
every citizen felt hope decaying

    don't shoot
    I am you

all of us have progenitors walking,
talking with us with hands on our shoulders
transferring generational strength and courage

ancestral language girds our groans
reminding us to carry on—
walk as millions, speak as one—
through the horrendous intentional lying, through the terror
of the innocent dying
resting and hallowed in eternal dignity
peace should also be for the living

human beings enjoying the ease of living
walking, jogging, driving, breathing

our ancestors know, they listen and
glow among the stars, tending to the
deprived and scarred

don't give up, don't give in
only together will humanity win

we *must* win
we must

we must win
we trust

they kiss us, console us
they see and encourage us to

keep living through the taunts
keep striving for what we want

even when the world says stop

Sea Legacy

I.
bodies jettisoned
float like canoes on a stream
their destination: Eden

II.
angry tones skim the
shoal of the unnamed sea   their
souls parade its floor

III.
the lawn: a field for
picnics and lynching
unsuspecting slaves

IV.
the mysteries smile
the pyramids don't crumble
the message: Universal

Yielding

if I am cursed
allow me to surrender
let the fight
drain from my grip
dousing hot flashes

varicose clusters
bunch at the bend
complicating the climb
towards consciousness

my October holds one hundred days
and I am at the center
pulling the new year towards me with
the might of the world's women

yelling to the past   *get back*
the tantrum of a two-year-old
fighting for her right to be

the ovum of now incubates
I balance, I breathe
and yield to thanksgiving
stripping away anything that
makes me anxious

now is mine
and I am hers

and in knowing
her yolk yields hope

U.S. of Birthing A.

tired and swollen
the mother remains patient
her baby's head's down

labor tells her to push
doctors say she doesn't know
where is the midwife

her body's design
ignored a birth at a time
rushed cesareans

she breastfeeds her son
no blanket to hide nature
pissed-off onlookers

The Brow and the Womb

If you know the Bible's stance
on the fall of man, then maybe you'll understand
the context of my question:

Do you find it odd
that women bear both punishments
spit by God?

the sweat of a man's brow
versus the pain of a woman's womb
transferrable degrees of suffering
versus the very birthing of humanity

Does anybody else see the dichotomy?

the perpetual cursing of the wonder-making
womb
the wondrous, magnificent, cursable womb
life-affirming energy
her resumé reads EVERYTHING

dumping her identity to wear his name
I do was the promise
not *I'll do it all*
oh the fall
the fall
the *cursable* fall

no this is not commentary on
equality or subserviency,
they are not the points in question
what begs your attention
is the question I mentioned

Do you find it kind of odd that
women bear both
punishments spit by God?

now China's Eve
America's Eve
Ghana's Eve
the world's Eve
all woke up and
found full wombs
pressed against wooden desks

let's review

she wears his name
deleting her identity that has kept her, shaped her
brought her to this day
screams every word that could be cursed
to bring forth his seed
then after six weeks turns
around and runs his establishment

she perpetuates the orbit

meanwhile, there are some men
who claim their punishment—
and many do a fairly good job,
yet we all can look in
some man's face through
the course of a day
and find that he is gainfully unemployed and happy
sitting back, watching the news
telling the women in his life what to do

but the Earth would need not produce
if women decided no pain would
ever squeeze our wombs, swell our breasts,
tease our youthful figures into denial

make road maps out of our veins
and turn hormonal changes into tennis matches

now don't get hot under the collar
this is a conversation starter

Do you find it odd
that women bear both punishments
spit by God?

Hot

I love
to don
my hands
with silver rings,
my brown skin peeking
through their delicate designs;
however, I think diamonds compliment
me more. I like to drink Welch's grape juice
no sugar added 'cause it makes my cheeks cry
and takes me down a path, through a village, up
a hillside, into a land where my grandmother to the
umpteenth power was queen, then I become her.

Nothing brings me more pleasure than sitting barely dressed in
the middle of a ninety degree day, body trying disparately
to cool me with its natural juices and me sipping on a
mason jar of hand-squeezed lemonade and my bare
toes digging into the cool earth beneath them
making toe cubby holes and then seeming
as a twist of nature an autumn breeze
hits my breasts and my nipples
freeze and I'm embarrassed
for a minute, but then
I find beauty in the
natural way of
things.

Always the One

she'd always put herself on a shelf
she was the elf in self

she'd always come running when others would fall
she was the all in call

she'd always defend while others would mend
she was the end in friend

she ended up giving what others would dish
she was the itch in bitch

Tip Top Worldwide: A Nod to KRS-One

The one before me

Was down with BDP

He said that if I could create

Well then I'd make some money

Ancestors set the pace

Now I'm running the race

The legacy b4 me oh no I'd never disgrace

He set the tone b4 self-destruction was born

Not the verb but the noun that had us singing along

See self-destruction was a rhyme in the stop the violence movement

Made you think about your life and the things that you was doing

There are those who believe in the power of the people

Then those who will never let the people be equal

Nevertheless we won't stress so much light out here to live

Now excuse me while I spit a few bars if you will

My initials are KJL

I write my thoughts

so my rhymes have a chance to sell

I take a little of this

and I take a little of that

sometimes I get bored

and pull my topics from a hat

graduated from university

so my rhymes might be in Japanese

tatoeba ichi ni san shi

watashi wa mecha ureshii

sometimes I like to walk

and sometimes I like to ride

but being from the D probably

I'll have to drive

sometimes I'm dressed to lounge

and sometimes I'm looking fly

how do I know dudes holla as I'm walking by

some people look at me

and see an African queen

some people look at me and see a sister from the streets

but when I see myself I see creativity

just want to be me and

still make some money

so people put your hands up if you're out here getting paid

so people get your hands up if you're out here getting paid

1, 2, 3...

I Write You When You Come

whenever and regardless 'cause
you tend to pop up like chat rooms and
sometimes retract like vacuum cords
just as I'm ready to explore you
you're through

your appearances and exits are unexpected
jarring me out of my sleep

I have no energy to jot you, so please stop you disrespectful
prose of brilliance
bookmark it please
let this epiphany
be the exhale in my morning stretch

but no,
you persist
so I reach for whatever's close
reading my nightstand like braille

nail polish, bobby-pin, cell phone, water glass

a napkin from Post and Beam wedged beneath
June Jordan's poetry
catching petals from
dying blue indigos
perfect to doodle you down on

where are you when I'm focused,
tucked in an afghan
poised with pen and pad in hand
green chai tea steeping on
the carved unity stand
watching blossoms of inspiration

sprouting from everything around me
polyester-blended skeins and djembes a framed
photograph from the
twenty-fifth family reunion

I wish you would orbit like rings
instead of shooting across my dreams like asteroids
you fly away and go and land on
another poet who
obliges you regardless of her setting, plot or conflict
she activates her wrist and
writes you when you visit

now I get to read my missed
opportunity in her masterpiece
the frustration, the frustration, the nauseating frustration

I get it

regardless the situation from which I'm drawn
I take a few moments and
I write you when you come

Somewhere Between Paragraphs

as soon as the words are written
someone will plunge below the lettering
pull their hair out in follicle clusters
cursing each strand as they curl around callused tips
there are some who drag their demons like
scalawags   worthless and foul but attached nonetheless

seraphim are just as likely
sauntering askance
phantasmagoria on any boulevard
in any backwards mirror on any block
witnesses to the days Buddha breathed

the lettering can't be everybody's net
some are too slick with pace and so they fall through
while others are unhinged with paranoia
and so their throats cling to the print and are asphyxiated

writing pleasures the wrist
a library of vocabulary etched in each bone
nostalgia painted in a museum of
tattered dolls and shoeboxes of yellowing letters
the lettering fades with each remembrance
causing you to forget to breathe

Beach Life

kelp tangles my feet
waves crash high knees and screeching
sandy burning eyes

jumping over waves
we left our lunch behind
seagulls flock to feast

running at top speed
playing catch with a football
bottoms come undone

plastic bottles roll
catching the sewer off guard
oceans spit them up

joggers on the shore
beach volleyball and bikers
dead swollen penguins

surfers catching waves
a sea lion steals the show
breathtaking sunset

each seashell I find
is especially for me
like my fingerprint

the Pacific here
is the same Pacific there
harsh wild and teeming

School Paper

the father heard the teacher say
his son's behavior was imbalanced
as the syntax left her lips
twitching swelled in the father's cheeks

his son kept his
gaze outside of the tattle-tailing

instead he watched his classmates
walk hand in hand with their parents
bubbling over with the best part of their day

the susurration of traffic and children squealing
cocooned the teacher and father's conversation

as he listened, his huge leathery palms squeezed the sides
of his son's small head, his callused thumbs pressed
into his temples

a fatherless touch from a father

the teacher missed the chance to protect her student, so his
little tense eyes caved to his father's crazed stare

the tattle-tailing was a sneeze the teacher wished
she had held
but as a sneeze
the molecules of information had
already reached the recesses of the crazed
man's mind

there were no scratches or bruises
to illustrate abuse and so it was not abuse

on paper that is

it was not abuse in the father's world for
his father used shoe heels and chair arms to
chisel sense into his small head   searing every
bitch in the book into his identity

fatherless words from a father

and now his grown eyes stitched with rage
choked his son's pleading gaze
grace was all her pupil wanted
pardon was what he petitioned
words he would later learn to spell
and fold into his vocabulary

overwrought eyes finally allowed the tears to fall
vulnerability his tattle-tailing teacher never saw
for he had to be his own father   yelling
no you can't share my crayons and
leave me alone, I'll line up when I get ready

the father told his son to tell his teacher he was sorry
and that it wouldn't happen again   but it wasn't the
words to which his son responded   but the increasing
pressure on his temples and so his small throat allowed
his apology to escape

and in that moment his eyes
shifted to those of his teacher's
she wondered why he was unusually
reserved and quiet

now her tattle-tailing told her

she watched as the two walked off
blending into the foot traffic
the teacher stood in the middle of hurrying

parents and giggling children
laden with culpability

her nerves quaked, her gut grew uneasy

and as surely as the fifth follows the fourth
her pupil arrived the next day
dressed in his usual reserve

as her eyes met his
amidst the bustling of her squealing students

a promise was made

and for two weeks after the tattle-tailing
he came to school everyday
some days willing to share and some days not

then he left her class
his father enrolled him in a different school

more often than not her concern was with her pupil
wondering if his new teacher would make the same
promise   hoping she would never need any paper

The Beauty of Morning

amber honey
black pepper
egg whites
pink salt
red onion
cherry tomatoes
arugula
Giovanni   Angelou
a word that is true to you
a window to look out of
a windowsill with mint and dill
there to trade with the neighbor's lemons

they've never been over for
breakfast or holiday
but they always wave

mornings are a bit sweeter when
folk are kind and caring

So Many People Ask

why does she settle
feeding the pull of the aching
caving to the yoke

she has to tiptoe
in a home she's paying for
eggshell covered floors

her slighted slapped face
swelling peridot imprint
slick with salty tears

she rubs in cold cream
wishing to live backwards
longing for before

when her laughs were strong
and her heart wasn't afraid
it tried to tell her

honeymoon flowers
on forced anniversaries
blank stares at the walls

lovers without words
sex left the conversation
soon separate rooms

married but alone
bound by mortgage and children
this is her *I do*

she stays up at night
attempting to calm her life
with a lullaby

her work is her calm
one shift done and one more left
dinner in the car

keeping step with time
a dance with obligation
witnessed by a rose

peacefully she leaves
grieving the woman she was
a new step with song

today she will know
how it feels to have the chance
to start all over

Peripatetic Being

I have trouble
staying in one place
I may be addicted to
needing new space

regardless the place
I make space
for my face
alight for a while
then back to my pace

a suitcase in case
I grow found of a place
along with a candle
a doily of lace
just enough vibe to
brighten the space

poems just in case
I grow fond of a face
fond of his thinking
fond of embrace

eventually I'll probably
settle in one place
my space
slowly
becoming
interrupting
pace

Storm

cold cruel stone
dust debating where to settle

opened backed gown
groans that never found comfort

pain that quieted dreams
swept away like kitchen floor mess

no siren to warn
just his blood running warm
and a sister glad to see her brother

it's that love that draws her to
the beach in search of his image
on the horizon

maybe one of these days
she'll spot his likeness

maybe one of these nights
the waves will conjure

the moon will guide
an he will step over that mountain range

she knows it sounds strange
but it makes her feel like she's still a sister

Her House

walls once white
are now mint green
mama, her sisters and children
pose in brass frames
proud to know a woman
grand warm and full
she has a foot hold on history
so a framed painting of
Frederick Douglass keeps watch

a partridge and peony chair
winged to hold up under laughter
when pigtails and ruffles were my style
floor pillows were the only invitation to
sit in the grown folk's room
in my stilettos and black jeans
I sit across from the winged chair
and count the memories it conjures

her jewelry box elegant and wooden
still willing to sing when wound
has always kept its place in
the room where I first learned
of my brother's passing
clocks that no longer keep time
no matter how grand
Sears Coldspot   thirty eight
years of turkey and cornbread dressing
collard greens and twice baked sweet potatoes
pie crusts and pickled peppers
Cha Cha and fried brown rice

my love of dobermans
came some twenty five years ago
when Tasha's eyes would glow

in the deep of the blue room
she was our racehorse
we'd put accent pillows on her back
and ride her around the kitchen family
room living room track

I'm old enough to remember the
yellow linoleum floors and
butterscotch shag carpeting
with a red sofa fit for company to sit
the family room was where the
dining room is now and the living room
always had a TV until recently

I'm old enough to remember
her red hair and square framed glasses and
when she wore the suits her hands made
she would make homemade sauerkraut and
churn vanilla ice cream
now arthritis has robbed her of her mothering

these days haven't been so kind
and we have reason to pause
stunned and frenzied in our respective states —
Michigan, California, Ohio, Alabama
trying our best to calm the panic

ending is happening and there is no handbrake for it
it's a selfish thought to consider one's
own suffering in the wake of a beloved's
decline   love can't help but pull in all directions

Her Hands

stirred and mixed
brought abundance
to the empty
a bountiful touch
made a quarter-full plenty

built and fixed
what most would leave broken
grabbed and gripped 'til
opportunity opened

sought and saved
as much as life would allow
worshipped and praised
hallelujah anyhow

gardened and cooked
anything that was available
not only set it, but could build
the dining room table

planted the seeds cleaned the greens
sewed the seams
provided, guided and chided
by righteous means

protested injustice
brought on by racism
pushed the vote
like an innate mechanism

her hands

paid, gave, suffered and saved
washed, bathed, buffered and made
prayed, aimed, achieved and claimed...

Victory

Remembrance

Grandma Jane's house
Mansfield, Ohio 1990
the phone rang

the call ended

Kyra she said
my feet hurried
Ivan is gone
He's with God

knees gave way
while hope faded
what's life now
live on, how

we headed home
Grandma Jane drove
rain and tears
cattle and cornfields

time kept crawling
all was falling
where was God
where was God

Detroit stood eerie
dreary cold roads
Grand River Longacre
two blocks home

we walked in
hollow chest racing

mama's sobbing cries
grief weak eyes

mama was broken
I was breaking
Lord have mercy
life had none

daddy prayed upstairs
pleading his faith
he was good
Ivan was good

pews, walls, aisles
massed with mourners
family filed in
hymns and flowers

remains lay tailored
mama bent over
caressed her son
goodbye my Ivan
goodbye my son

my beloved slept
church folk wept
friends and family
cried then left

ashes to ashes
dust to dust
return to God
be with God

best big brother
I still remember
always with me
more than memories

I live fearlessly
because of you
Thank you Ivan
I love you

fly   Ivan   fly

Tiptoe

some days I cartwheel the tightrope

others I tiptoe my way   slow

keep my scope off the world below

set on where I gotta go

maneuver through the ebb and flow

my walk   it ain't done for show

just getting where I gotta go

don't matter if I'm fast or slow

mostly speed ain't the way to go

so I tiptoe the tightrope

thankful for the peace I know

not concerned about what's below

no-handed cartwheel   that's a show

went fast now I'm going slow

did my stunt now I lay low

tiptoeing where I gotta go

Expectation

I did not expect to awaken to this

shut down and gone
suggesting lengths of time I needed
to figure out my life

another unavailable one
the kind who love to finger and fuck

the women they've loved
are bland so they
become addicted to the
lure

trysts birthed out of need
so pure so pure

we wallowed
in chemistry
matrimony never gave

the purring of intimacy
the groan of the empty

I am empty
and so is he

slipping beneath
all that is sane and holy

never having heard the heartbeat
of lovers who loved us
crumbling beneath the need to trust

lips that kiss and seduce
filtered commitment blistering
unsure unsure

loneliness unexpected
I awakened left to figure out
my life alone

{2 hours pass}

this is so pathetic
this loneliness unexpected

this loud gnawing mood
so boisterous so rude

this vacant availability
you'll never have the best of me

never 'cause you're blocked
blockety blocked blocked blocked

delete delete delete
he'll be the one who misses me

who does he think I am
he can't know who I am

at this point it doesn't matter
his dreams with me are shattered

get out of my life with your sophomoric tomfoolery
you walking poster of swap meet jewelry
you'll never have the likes of me

I don't think he was aware
he was the one without a pass
thinking his mediocre attempt at love would last

no sir not today
I've chosen to stay disgruntle
and alone
forever

{the next morning}

he'll call..

{unblocked}

Aftertaste

reminiscing be cozy like sofas
looking back like Sankofa

I never told you this
but I appreciated you when
you were around

we held it down and together
like book ends
lit like wicks
tight knit like cross stitch

you were my friend
would have done anything for you

we had memories
old like yearbooks and mixtapes
with notes being
passed in the back of the class

would pick you first
and give you my last

you were my friend

you never knew
but I thought the
world of you

but
one of those sacred
seven year cycles

flipped us so hard
we couldn't see each other

didn't miss each other
and so we found others

a beautiful photo left in the rain fades
doesn't mean it was never beautiful
just means the heart has to carry it now

the stories we shared
the dreams we dared
the strength of being there
until we were nowhere

all of this life that's been lived
gets in the way

all of the whispering wounds say
keep the bond at bay

but I appreciated you
and loved you like family
and now there is
peace with the distance

absence makes the familiar strange sometimes
a desire to embrace and a need for goodbye
sometimes that lifetime line is a lie

whatever your life entails
be well
and know that you were loved

Gravity

he says my voice is his symphony
and my lips   his favorite literature

hums the lyrics of my eyes
hits the keys of my waistline

turns my pain into ashes
I inhale him like Sanchez

versatile and kind
pliable in his mind
when days zoom like seconds
he just slows down time

never thought I would find him
so considerate and nice when
other men had me spiraling
opened his heart and said *come in*

he   man he is something else
beyond the thrills I've ever felt

digs my art and conversation
I've got nothing but appreciation

he's fine and he gets me
leads ever so gently
he fills where I'm empty
leans in and says simply

I'll love you forever if you let me

and with that I let go
gave thanks and fell slow

he has the patience and audacity
to love me past capacity
a steady pull that balances me
he is my gravity

Tegami

I turn my pillow over

so the slob-free smooth

side can show company

how neatly and nicely I sleep

I find a folded note — purple

'cause you know it makes

my skin dance   my heart

feels your hands' caress as I

gently pull its edges apart

and release the *love you*

left me

Detour

just as I pass

on the way to my creator's palm

I will take a thousand years to roam

ride the rings of Saturn

gaze into Jupiter's spot

Mercury will beg me to be her moon

and Venus   her constellation

I will wrap my energy around

the sun's and tell her what

a blessing she is

out there where there are no endings

just endless beginnings

I will choose to be

a light beam lined with lavender

Sunbird

a
sunbird
sips
from
a
Sisibi
tree
*

her
wings
fluttering
with
the
poise
of
a
dream
*

she
watched
under
the
Sisibi
tree
dreaming
of
a
day
she
would
be
free
*

she
is
powerful
and
delicate
and
elegant
a
kindred
image
of
you